MEMORIA

poems

MEMORIA

ORLANDO RICARDO MENES

LOUISIANA STATE UNIVERSITY PRESS BATON ROUGE

Published with the assistance of the
University of Notre Dame, Notre Dame, Indiana

Published by Louisiana State University Press
Copyright © 2019 by Orlando Ricardo Menes
All rights reserved
Manufactured in the United States of America
LSU Press Paperback Original

DESIGNER: Mandy McDonald Scallan
TYPEFACE: Calluna
PRINTER AND BINDER: LSI

Library of Congress Cataloging-in-Publication Data

Names: Menes, Orlando Ricardo, author.
Title: Memoria : poems / Orlando Ricardo Menes.
Description: Baton Rouge : Louisiana State University Press, [2019]
Identifiers: LCCN 2018034712| ISBN 978-0-8071-6941-4 (pbk. : alk. paper)
| ISBN 978-0-8071-6942-1 (pdf) | ISBN 978-0-8071-7063-2 (epub)
Classification: LCC PS3563.E52 A6 2019 | DDC 811/.54—dc23
LC record available at https://lccn.loc.gov/2018034712

for my wife Ivis and our two children,
Valerie and Adrian

Everything brought back sounds of the past,
of an ancient forest that no longer existed.
Even the light in that grove was like a memory
of light.

—RAFAEL ALBERTI
The Lost Grove (translated by Gabriel Berns)

What you remember saves you. To remember
Is not to rehearse, but to hear what never
Has fallen silent.

—W. S. MERWIN
"Learning a Dead Language"

CONTENTS

MEMORIA

Kissing in Madrid

Dance floor of Rex, Gran Vía discotheque,
My first deep-tongue kiss, sloppy, succulent
Like mango, long slurps, giggly burps, my neck
Wet with nibbles, as we grope, grind, vent
Libido, strobes pulsing to Barry White's moan,
Our bodies simmering in slow-burn funk,
She an Air Force brat from the base at Torrejón,
Frizzy blonde, light as a mannequin, I the clunk
In platforms, bell-bottoms tight as a corset,
So I cling to her, swaying in that nicotine fog,
No words to spoil such a gift of spit and sweat
Given to a boy she's just met, shy, bookish, a clog
With seduction, and once the song is done,
We split, lurch, mouths dry, lips like laundry wrung.

Photo Booth

I never knew when Mamá would sneak
in my room to search for pills, pot, model glue,
or flip through my LPs & trash any with covers
that made her screech & bang her forehead,
especially *They Only Come out at Night*
with a bejeweled Edgar Winter in makeup
thick as stucco, his band in glam polyester suits
like macaws preened for Rio's *carnaval*.

One day Mamá poked inside Alice
Cooper's *Love It to Death* & found a fresh
strip of black & whites with my pants down,
no briefs, I'd taken in a street booth,
a prank my buddies & I played on a Sunday
to shock the girls in Ventas near the bullring.

Mamá shrieked, her hand slapping the dresser.
"Who's that man? Is he your lover?
Are you an invert like those singers you adore?"
"No, no, it's only me," I plead. "It can't be.
You're just a boy," she replied. "I swear
it's the truth. I can't stop thinking about girls,"
I said. "Prove it & drop your pants," she demanded.
"You're crazy," I yelled, then ran out the house,
roamed the streets, got back after midnight
when the doorman let me in since I'd left my keys.

Mamá said nothing the next morning, nor days later
to Papá when he returned from a business trip.
I can't say why she didn't tear up & flush the strip
(I was the one who burned it in the kitchen sink),
but from then on Mamá became the Torquemada
of sissies (or those vulnerable to sissyhood like me).

She hammered & sheared to bits my brogues
with the eight-inch heels, slapped if she saw my arms
akimbo, tongue-lashed when my legs crisscrossed
soft & sweet like the scissors of a seamstress.
Be a man, a real man, & bend that right leg into
an angle, true & hard-edged as a carpenter's square.

Macho

From the Latin *masculus,* male,
as in a pipe threaded on the outside
that screws into the inner thread
of its opposite called female, *la hembra,*
as in the stud that mounts the mare,
as in the three-stage rocket that pierces
our placental atmosphere.

I first heard the word from Mamá
when she shamed me (I must've been ten
or eleven) for being timid, emotional,
running to her in tears whenever
cracker boys shot me with their BB guns.

A boy who isn't macho is just a girl
with a weenie, she'd say or think
(so long ago I can't remember which,
but does it really matter, anyway?).

A real man, *un macho de verdad,*
punches and kicks to break bones
(bruises are just downright sissy),
who stomps and bellows so hard
even the walls tremble, who eats
iron nails and shits nuclear grenades.

Next time you hear "macho man,"
forget about the Village People's
happy-go-lucky disco song about leather
dudes who lust after Indian chiefs
in the bathhouses of Castro Street.

No, no, it's the other Castro
you should be thinking about, our Fidel,
our Fidelito, our Fidelazo,
macho of machos, bellower of bellowers,
the beastly bull that raped our island
(*la isla*/feminine), our cannibal Minotaur
with testicles like bunker busters,

our tyrant of tyrants whose phallus
hovers like the longest cannon ever
made (as in Hitler's or Saddam Hussein's)
from Punta Maisí to Punta Hicaco,

our nuclearly hetero caudillo
who sent gays to concentration
camps with big metal signs that read
"Work Will Make You a Man."

Sharing a Meal with the Cuban Ex-Political Prisoners

Colony Hotel, South Miami Beach, 1993

A pileup of black pots, clay pans on a tile table,
nine guests cramped on low stools—
milk crates—cold drinks between our legs to calm

the tiny man who'd been tortured
with ice water, another guy, phobic of things
metallic, using a plastic spork from 7-Eleven.

The fried pork is suck-to-the-bone good, but I quit
eating when Saúl, our host, fiancée's classmate,
starts to describe his years at La Cabaña
where he lost one kidney to pesticides in the well,

one eye spooned out, liver stuck with knitting needles.
How time got lost without clocks, bells,
calendars, roosters, his own heartbeat in disarray.

Just as I take the fork again, Saúl expounds
on pain, his power to numb nerves, gums, joints,
stretch skin like a rubber sail, harden the skull
to titanium. More men tell their stories of rape

by German shepherds in hospital rooms,
having to march wearing wool socks with glass,
the loud machine that took out toenails.

I cannot stop sweating, shaking, fiancée poking,
what's wrong with you, show respect,
these men are brave, which makes me more nervous.
I swoon in the bathroom, my skull pains

with their screams, throbbing image of a little man
frantic in a ballroom of funhouse mirrors,
convex phantasms, gun pops, flush of voices,
his head butting glass to make the nightmare stop.

Camp

The fascists were no doubt brutal but also
ingenious as when early in the war
Nationalist pilots would drop fragile supplies
(nitro? hypos? death sentences?) in boxes
dangling from legs of flapping turkeys,
which took care of dinner for the troops

since no one can eat a parachute. How absurd,
you might say, but isn't truth stranger
than fiction? Indeed, a dollop of creative
conjecture might well serve the truth better
than scrupulous attention to the facts.

Imagine that the filmmaker Pedro Almodóvar
were a bona fide historian who's written
the definitive book on the Spanish Civil War.
Dominican nuns would be suicide bombers,
their black habits just as stealthy as burkas.

Schoolgirls would sneak into church
disguised as altar boys, tie up the priest
with jumping ropes, then vandalize the altar
putting makeup on the dying Christ,
plus curly wig, silk stockings, and brassiere.

Or, better yet, Franco's shock troops,
the Moors and legionnaires, would instead
be a battalion of transvestites with blonde bouffants,
names like Sgt. Kiki and Major Madelaine,
who camp in Matahari tents spritzed
with French perfume, velvet pillows to rest
their pedicured feet. They'd storm the trenches
around Madrid in Gucci gowns, Prada pumps,

seducing communist militias with nougat
Mausers, egg-cream grenades, bonbon kisses,
and in a hail of rockets they'd all get married
by the Generalissimo himself dressed as a cardinal
(or a matador?) playing a flamenco guitar
as every cloud in the sky explodes to meringue.

Matador

That pretty suit of lights I wear to please the fans befits more the trapeze boy who teases death with giggles because he knows there's a net below. What makes a man a man is brash brio, reckless, primal. Isn't fear of death the sugar that sweetens life? A real torero, macho to the marrow, faces the bull naked, barefoot, no loincloth or sissy sandals. What about that silly cape? Sew it into a flamenco skirt. Those soft slippers? Put them on a ballerina's feet. And the hosiery? Give it away to the little biddies at church. No warm sand but live coals for me, a ring of fire with barbwire bushes, the crowd hurling gibes instead of roses. Manhood demands martyrdom. I stand straight before the wily beast, my legs strong as war pikes as the beast's hair chafes my skin, and I soon see its drool gleaming like a silver chalice in the sun, our Spanish sun so strong, so manly in daylight, before it runs away, a coward beneath the skirts of night.

My Father's Pantry

Despensa in Spanish, from *dispensus,*
meaning well-apportioned,
and yours was copious, Papá,
your inalienable domain
where you hung chorizos
dribbling smoky grease,
blood-and-rice sausages
big as cast-iron pipes,
your prize ham, *pata negra,*
from those acorn-fed black pigs
of Salamanca,
a whole leg coddled for years
in salt's sacrament,
mottled skin supple as vellum,
sweet bone to crack
for garbanzo stew.
How I loved the smell
of your larder in the morning,
sausages pulsing with spice,
perspiring paprika—
your lair, your cave, your underworld
of charcuterie
and Cuban cigars that took on
that dry-cured taste
you cherished
as you drank old Scotch,
which is when you told stories
of growing up so poor
that hairy cracklings were a feast.
It is food, you'd say,
more than time itself that heals
the pain of poverty.
Perhaps that's why you found grace

carving ham in its steel rack,
your long, pliant knife
slicing off the marbled meat
thin as hosts.

Judo

"Judo will make you a man, stop you from sulking
in your mother's closet," Papá would say
as he took me, just turned twelve, to that small dojo
by the bodega on Douglas and Flagler Street

where Sensei—a blond, blue-eyed Cuban
with a flattop and the granitic face of Charles Bronson—
swung us by the collar into maelstroms

of *osotogari* (the trip or reap), *ippon seoi nage*
(the shoulder flip), and other throws
I refused to do even if his garlic mouth
got in my nose or his toenails dug into my butt.

I hated his cubanazo swagger, like a gunslinger
doing the rumba on a muggy day,
hated how he wore no underwear to show off his manhood,
hated too how he shook, pinched us
in those potato-sack uniforms that stank of our sweat and our tears.

What a thrill to disobey with a cause,
to be a martyr for freedom as he called me prison meat
when I threw my yellow belt into the trash can
as the other boys gawked in silence.

Sensei glared, snarled, reamed his fist
into the palm of another hand, but didn't smack me.
He declared my expulsion to everyone,
said I was worse than Fidel and his bearded thugs.

Scrunched in a corner of the plastic tatami,
I waited for Papá to pick me up, who after hearing
the teacher's fulminations, just told me
to get in the car and keep quiet as a corpse. I feared
he was going to belt me or at least scold me
but all he did was stare at the road in his mirrored sunglasses
as we drove back home on South Dixie Highway.

The Man with No Name

after Sergio Leone's *A Fistful of Dollars,* perhaps my father's favorite movie

Trigger, hammer, barrel are my trinity, the three beats to my revolver's song. Not hollow words like faith, hope, and charity. Just horseshit to me. To believe is to be deceived. I trust my Navy Colt .38 as much as the farmer trusts his plow. Seven and a 1/2 inches on a smoke-wagon barrel, coiled rattlesnake on the grip. Let the plowman sow Indian corn in the stony earth. I sow lead in the flesh of men, bad or good matters none to me. I am the widow maker, the orphan multiplier. Their tears are my rain, their sighs my wind. Marriage is no sacrament to me. I honor the coffin maker, but I have no use for gabby preachers. They just say pretty words and make hocus-pocus with their hands. Call me Paul of the Projectile. Death is the good news I spread with the twitch of an eye and a swift hand. My fury has a slow fuse, like the cigarillo I suck from the corner of my mouth—so sweet, so bitter I remember that Sunday when a mob of birds tolled a church bell right when a horse thief was being hung from a hickory tree.

You've got that crazy feelin' now now now
You've got that crazy feelin'
You've got that crazy feelin' deep inside
    —LOU REED, "Crazy Feeling"

They fuck you up, your mum and dad.
  They may not mean to, but they do.
They fill you up with the faults they had
  And add some extra, just for you.
    —PHILIP LARKIN, "This Be the Verse"

Doctor Lu

Orlandito filched from potpourri drawers his aunt's
creamy pantyhose in plastic eggshells, rayon undies
& padded bras he wrapped around his knees,
squeezing & grinding the you-know-what between his legs.

Hoarded under his fold-up cot they'd soon smell
of overripe plantains (the bedroom next to the kitchen);
he did the you-know-what anywhere he sniffed
plátanos maduros fritos—his classroom at La Luz School,

Clínica Pasteur on Calle Ocho, even Saint John Bosco's Church
as Padre Ruiz sermonized on Cain's exile to the wilderness.
One Sunday after taking communion, he began to lock
himself in the bathroom, hoping steamy water

might cloud God's angry gaze. One Lenten Saturday
when he'd forgotten to lock the door, his mother caught him
naked with a girdle between his legs. Slapping & praying,
she called him *degenerado,* burned the secret lingerie.

Distrustful of priests & psychiatrists, she took her boy
to Juan Lu, chino cubano, who can cure any malady.
Orlandito trembled on the steel table as Doctor Lu examined
genitals, "too small for his age," he said. "Self-stimulation had caused

excess skin to stick to the glans. Cases like this result
in atrophy, organ that's good only to urinate." Legs raised,
mouth biting rubber, his foreskin was stretched back
until it almost appeared circumcised. Eyeliner running,

voice crackling, his mother blessed El Chino Eminente,
thanking him for saving her firstborn son. "A man
who isn't a man should be shot like a lame horse.
Even priests procreate." Orlandito shuffled home sore,

nauseated, chunk of ice inside his pants. "God punishes
vices. Touch your little tail once more & you'll have
to squat to pee." Steel heels hammer the terrazzo floor,
clicks & pings echo through the Lysol-smelling lobby.

Pirates World

Like the young St. Teresa who almost ran off
With her brother to be martyred in the land
Of Moors, I too tried but failed to hitch a ride
North to Pirates World in Dania, my first
Concert ever, the Alice Cooper band, a long
Ways (thirty miles) from Calle Ocho.

I was still fourteen, the road full of danger
Even by day, Mamá warned, with perverts
Lurking at every corner, those married men
Cruising in their leather-upholstered Impalas,
Giving out roofies, asking, *Need a ride
To the mall? Wanna have lunch at Burger King?*
So I guess it was fear, as usual, that kept me
From hearing Alice Cooper sing in his creepy
Baritone "I'm Eighteen," "School's Out,"
"My Stars," and my favorite, "Dead Babies."

O Alice, I missed you in your ripped leotards,
Dirty top hat and leopard-skin boots,
Your face with runny black make-up like a widow
Who's just buried her husband in the rain.
Come take me away from Little Havana
And its musty bodegas, barbershop dungeons,
North to the real America of Twinkies and tater tots,

Where boys are free of curfews, prying crucifixes,
Your big wheels grinding past the swamps
And the bayous, past the cornfields and the silos,
West to Amarillo where the rodeo girls kiss
With marshmallow lips, and a boy's mouth
Fills with warm molasses, so many Mary Lous
And Annie Maes with butterscotch eyes, rosy skin
To love on long hayrides, banjos in the breeze.

Rock 'n' Roll Animal

after Lou Reed's live LP from 1974

Cropped head, whitewashed face, O Lou, our goth-butch apostle
In skintight leather pants, eagle's-head buckle on a rhinestone belt,
Your black lips sneering punk as you sang of dime-bag dealers
With wingtip shoes & Times Square queens in paisley blousons,

Your dog collar glinting S&M to kids in straitlaced homes,
Our mothers horrified to have borne sons so twisted, so perverse,
Their mop sticks primed to beat us into Marlboro Men,
("Why can't you boys listen to Nat King Cole or Tom Jones?"),

So we hid you in the darkest places, those lost cupboards
& lonely closets, taking you out when alone in the house
To spin "Sweet Jane" & "Heroin" on plastic phonographs,
Butcherly lo-fi, so loud those mono speakers got the DTs,

Sonic swells breaching our eardrums, overflowing our brains,
O how we soared into red-poppy skies when those twin guitars,
Dick's & Steve's, took turns spiking the air with barbwire riffs,
Amputated melodies (& don't forget Prakash John's deadpan bass),

While you sang into your silver mike of doomsday picnics
In Central Park, *the politicians making crazy sounds,*
The bodies piled up in mounds . . . O those fucked-up words,
Those downbeat rhymes that made rainbows of our rage.

Radio Luxembourg

Late at night when reception was best,
Bivouacked under the sheets of my fold-up bed,
I'd aim my transistor's taped antenna

Northward to the strongest FM station
In Europe (British despite the name)
And hear whole records by prog-rock bands

With the weirdest names: Atomic Rooster,
Spooky Tooth, King Crimson, Pink Floyd,
Van Der Graaf Generator, Hawkwind,

Rare as truffles in those department store bins
Where *Sgt. Pepper's* and *Goats Head Soup*
Were the edgiest LPs a Spanish kid could get.

Like some fishbowl guppy thrown to sea,
I reeled for the first time to a saxophone's
Spiral eddies, bounced on wakes of electric bass,

Rode the mellotron's loopy waves in a storm
Of riffs plucked from amped-up Superstrats
Vibrating every proton of my bony body,

& I heard the Floyd's "Echoes" call to me
At 1 a.m. (or was it 3 or 4, who really knows,
I'd taken caffeine pills to stay awake).

"Jump, jump into the deep," the chorus sang,
& I sank down, down, so many seismic chugs,
Zinging diatoms, zapping protozoa, sea-monkeys

Howling, an armada of panchromatic whales
Pinging mating calls to midget submarines,
Stingrays of guitar swirling to purple haze.

Am I a boy? Am I fish? I am a bathyscaphe
Of love in an ocean of love, & I bob, bop,
Boogie down with viperfish, vampire squid,

Kiss the radioactive siren whose dreadlocks
Sting & burn, whose beaky mouth sucks me
Inside out into a crumple of happy nothingness.

Tarkus

Emerson, Lake, and Palmer's LP from '71
I'd play over and over in black light—

Matte cover of an egg-hatched, double-barreled,
World War I Mark V-style armadillo tank.

A bunker-headed grasshopper with missiles.
A red-eyed pterodactyl with turbofan jets.

How Keith's synthesizer opens slowly
Like the napalm sun that dawns on Vietnam.

Greg's bass pops into those cluster bombs
Above the rice paddies and the straw huts.

Carl's drums pound the soft clouds
To rain down blood and bile on every village

As the war plays out on our color TVs,
Daily counts of the dead and wounded,

So many grunts lost to smack, opium too,
Technicolor coffins floating to heaven

At Moog speed, then a quick cut to
Tony the Tiger and his Frosted Flakes,

And back to some four-star general
Assuring us how Agent Orange will defoliate

Those evil Asian jungles to kingdom come,
Plus another break to Charlie the Tuna,

Then back again to the Green Berets
Killing communist cannibals in the Mekong,

Hordes of Hueys strafing the VCs
In rackety riffs, full-metal jacket—

How soon, so very soon General Patton,
Our Star-Spangled Antichrist in Ziggy Stardust duds,

Will come back to this wicked world,
Fire the laser cannon of his monster Sherman

Fast as a desperado shoots a Colt Peacemaker,
And end war once and for all, amen.

Stones #1

Most discos played ABBA and the Bee Gees
for Francoist youth to dance in their Sunday best,
but Stones #1 was our cathedral of rock and roll,
be it acid, hard, psychedelic, boogie, or proto-punk—

strobes high in the nave, velvet icons of Hendrix and Morrison
on paneled walls, tabernacled Les Pauls and Stratocasters,
a purple-lit pulpit decaled with Jagger's lips and tongue
from which English DJs spun the latest 45s and LPs.

Every Friday night misfit kids like me would flock
through her steel doors buzzed on beer and wine
from the dingy bars around La Latina to stomp, bang,
scrunch to Black Sabbath, Slade, Led Zeppelin.

Boys who shred air guitars wore military boots,
the howlers snakeskin platforms like Bowie's Ziggy.
I was more bohemian with my Indian tunic,
stiff Wranglers, square-tipped boots, and I tended to move
with soul, Motown style, which made no sense.

Girls preferred wool miniskirts with silk blouses
but not the one we called Bennie (from Elton's song)
because she always wore black leather pants,
silver platform boots, and a tight red turtleneck—
her pageboy hair-sprayed stiff as a helmet.

Bennie never talked, never smiled, danced alone
with stern cat eyes, spangled lips. One time
when the speakers boomed "Smoke on the Water,"
Bennie pulled three boys to the middle
of the floor, and I followed, some girls too,

then we drifted into a circle, sweaty, out of breath,
hopping and hoofing to the drumbeat,
howling to the squeals of lead guitar, our arms
flailing as we swayed, throbbed to organ waves—
free O so free like jellyfish in a Devonian sea.

St. Stanislaus Kostka School

Our campus neither dour nor majestic like Philip II's Escorial (a short ride away on that
Treeless plateau of rabbits, crows, Civil War shrapnel) but cold in a corporate

Way—dull steel, drab glass, dun concrete, quick to pit, crumble, unlike granite,
Imperial stone. My classmates were sons of generals and grandees with gilded

Lineages, boys who killed time at country clubs in their pressed Lacoste Polos,
Button-fly Levis, penny (peseta!) loafers, chain-smoking Winstons or Marlboros

Down to the sludgy filter, clicked aflame with lacquered lighters from Germany.
Cepero and I were the only stateside Cubans, his parents Freedom Flight refugees

Working two factory jobs each to send him abroad so he'd stay away from gangs
In the Bronx, my own father, store owner in hock, who hid when the creditors rang.

Papá took out collateral loans to pay my tuition, showed me off to his friends as a star
Pupil when in fact I got poor grades, F's in Latin (those loathsome declensions). It felt better

To sneak out from class with Cepero and Segura, nouveau-riche Murcian, to smoke
Dark-leafed Habanos, lung busters, macho tabaco. The first boy who choked

Got knuckled in the arm, jeered as a pansy, so we told tall tales about foreign
Girls, tall, blonde Nordics, though Cepero's were true as he lived alone in a pensión

By Puerta del Sol, popular with German backpackers, guiltless girls for whom sex
Was good clean fun if done with a condom, while *las españolas* would get their heads

Smashed with a frying pan if their mothers found out they were no longer virgins,
Fathers too who belted them for breaking curfew, the absolute 10 p.m. of fascist Spain,

But some girls rebelled, rockers like Margarita who wore hobnailed boots, white
Tanks with no bra, patched pants, her black hair feathered. We'd meet at twilight

In Plaza Mayor where hippies drank bota wine, danced, kissed, sang Beatles songs
To untuned guitars, clay drums, until the cops in gray stormed us with batons,

But we outran them on the cobbles, hands entwined, screams of joy, as we sped
Against time, free of adult burdens, life's humdrum hardships, the tyranny of should.

El Rastro

South of Plaza Mayor by Plaza de Cascorro—
past streets named Lettuce, Raisin, Barley—
is Madrid's outdoor market called El Rastro,
hundreds of stalls, lean-tos, tents squeezed tight

as niches where anything from a clawfoot tub
to a surgeon's saw to a tattered *La Celestina*
bound in sheepskin could be haggled down
with raunchy bravado or the promise of beer.

Mostly it was junk passed off to the tourists
as pricey souvenirs, like plastic castanets, hand fans
of silk (rayon really), or tin-plate doubloons.
So what drew the youth of Madrid to this place

every Sunday afternoon by the hundreds?
None of us were bargain hunters or hoarders,
just hippieish kids in patched dungarees,
espadrilles, & wool coats frayed to cheesecloth,

our pockets with enough pesetas to buy
a handful of stale cigarettes. It was to revel
in life, squeeze out joy from the lees of fate,
make fellowship like pilgrims to a shrine.

We'd sprawl against a wall or a lamppost
long into the afternoon to talk, joke, carouse,
eat cheese rinds with secondhand bread,
drink wine more like iodine than merlot,

oblivious to time & space, the crowds tripping
on our legs, tossing butts into our heads,
how they smelled like horses & we told them so,
who then shot out crude medieval curses,

but we didn't care, for we felt alive as never before,
singular in every breath, word, & thought,
stubborn as wayward seeds that trick a drought
& grow into hardscrabble woodland trees.

Autostop

It was a sunny afternoon of processions
in Guadalajara, which in Spain means food, drink,
boys fighting young bulls with cropped horns.
By dusk I had spent my last pesetas, my train ticket
to Madrid somehow soaked with spilled beer.
So I hitched a ride—*autostop*—at a Repsol station
on the N-320, and got picked up by a cramped,
pug-nosed SEAT 600, tinier than a VW bug
with muddy wrenches and pipes tossed in the back,
a red rosary coiled around the rear-view mirror,
holy cards glued to a dusty, crinkled dashboard.
The driver, a gray-haired, thick-browed man
in blue coveralls, shouted, "Where are you going?"
I said, "Madrid." "*Vale,*" he nodded, his eyes red, crotch wet,
and I slid into a seat that sank in the middle.
The car lurched, gears ground, wove in and out
the yellow lines, and he took long swigs
from a green bottle between his legs, asked where I was from,
what I was doing in Spain, his speech slurred, his lips
chapped and creased. I sputtered some answers,
"I'm a Cuban from Miami. My *abuelos* were *españoles,*" etc.
My hands shook as I gripped the sides of the seat,
my eyes fixed on the dark road ahead
as the car continued to weave and stammer.
The man named Joselín, swigging some more, told me
in-between profanities how much he hated
los yanquis, will never forget they shot his grandfather
in Cuba, wished they'd get nuked by the Soviets.
The car began to swerve, zig-zag, bump against
something (tire treads, a muffler, a vulture, or a hare,
I don't know), other cars honking, trucks bellowing,
yells of "I shit on your mother who's a whore."
I grabbed the wheel, turned fast to the right, avoiding a van
in the opposite lane, and screamed, Stop, stop, stop.

Joselito let go of the pedal and the car choked
onto the swale, my legs trembling so much
I could feel the muscles twitch and spike,
both of us crossing ourselves several times.
For a long while we said nothing, the only sound
that of tattered trucks. Then Joselito cried
about his wife betraying him with another plumber,
his best friend since they were kids growing up
in a small town in La Mancha, how he broke
the guy's leg with a monkey wrench one night
when the neighbors began to whisper *cornudo,*
fingers making horns, as he passed them on the stairs.
I shared my own break-up stories, so silly
both of us laughed. We hugged like father and son,
smoked the last Fortunas, drank the bottle dry,
then at some point dozed off until the sun
sobered us awake, our eyes crusty, mouths dry.
We cranked the SEAT 600 back to life,
had coffee and warm bread by the roadside,
then sailed in silence on the asphalt currents
to Madrid's Puerta del Sol, our little car
gliding like a caravel to this Gate of the Sun,
Spain's navel, point zero, her alpha and omega,
where the empire was born and died,
where every road and every life begins and ends.

Mr. Cossio, My Ninth-Grade English Teacher

After just a year studying in London
at one of those academies on the West End,
you taught us the Queen's English

at St. Kostka where you sashayed
in your strawberry Oxford shirt, wool slacks
of warm cream fastidiously creased,

a peach tweed jacket whose brass buttons
you'd fidget with every time I spoke too fast
and you tripped up trying to tag along.

Yes, you had impeccable grammar, unlike me.
You could name every British monarch
from Elizabeth I to II. But I alone had practiced

to perfection the jaw-breaking schwa
of Middle America with Lou's *newyok* slang,
so my classmates snickered I should teach

the class instead, which made me feel special,
but it was you, Mr. Cossio, who reached out
to me, the cocky cubanito and wannabe americano,

lending me your prim Penguin paperbacks
—*Animal Farm* and *Catcher in the Rye*—
I took home and devoured by night, whose words

saturated my senses, gushed into my mind,
pinched my soul, an ecstasy I'd never had before
reading Dr. Seuss or the *World Book* encyclopedia,

even if I had to look them up on every page—
so many cloistered thoughts, fears, and desires
given voice, amplified, made hallow in these books,

and I understood for the first time
how words are like ore that when forged and honed
with grace will pierce a stubborn heart.

Talking to Lou Reed: A Boy's Homage

You hit me with a flower,
Lou, a plastic daisy,
because life is a big fat lie,
and that's why I wear
huge wooden heels
'cause they make me feel
like I'm a man,
a tall and strong
Clint Eastwood
kind a guy
who could *stick* his *tongue*
in some girl's *ear,*
and she'd boogie with joy,
then marry him just like that,
no job, no car, just beer
money in his pocket.

Hey the other day
in Plaza Mayor
I met a chubby blonde girl
from Wyoming
who lassoed wild ponies,
tamed bears with apricots,
so *very regal to me*
we shared a wedge
of Manchego in the shade,
so *nice,* such *paradise,*
we laughed and kissed
when I spilled sangria
on my crotch. *A perfect day,*
don't you think?
But you're right,
of course,
love is phonier than Velveeta
on Wonder Bread,

and soon after she left for Ibiza
with an Icelandic sailor
old enough to be her dad,
a greasy-haired guy with pimples everywhere,
but the finest crocodile boots
and a long Afghan coat with epaulets,
which made me more angry than sad.

Only you, Lou, not my mom,
not my dad know how it feels
to hunt for love in a world of lies,
the near, the half, and the full,
all the same to me, and I feel
so *sick and dirty, more dead than alive*
that I swallow Mom's valium
late at night by the subway stop
or mix white wine with gin
in the slimy bars of Lavapiés
where the drunk legionnaires
beat their hairy chests
and never ask for love, grace,
or anything big from the world.

Blood

Rather than hauling sacks
of flour for beer money
in the dry docks around Vallecas,
I found easy work as an interpreter
for a moving company
on La Gran Vía that had a contract
with the US Air Force
at their base in Torrejón de Ardoz,

where zoomie families lived in
ranch houses with clean-cut lawns,
picket fences, wide driveways
for pickup trucks and muscle cars.
Most *madrileños* had to squeeze
into dark cubbyholes, gray tenements
with sidewalks narrow as ledges
where tiny cars wallowed for weeks,
dinged, bashed, famished for gas.

I got paid twice a worker's wage
for labeling boxes and pieces of furniture,
kitchenware, records, books, etc.,
but the harder part, way beyond my abilities,
was bridging that ancient divide
between the Anglo and Hispanic worlds,
a clash of civilizations acted out
not in grand sea battles or long sieges
but every time an Air Force guy
said Spaniards were lazy, stupid, smelly,
and refused to let the workers
use the bathroom or give them water
to drink in the heat of summer.

I should have been a mediator, a healer
as someone who straddled both worlds
(didn't I love hot dogs and malted milk,
speak English like a kid from Kalamazoo?),
but instead I felt the rage I once had
as the sole Hispanic boy in Mrs. Weaver's
fourth-grade class where I was taunted
and roughed up by the chain-link fence.

In revenge, I mislabeled as many boxes
as I could, such as bric-a-brac for pillows, etc.
When lunch came and I told the workers
what I'd done, they raised their glasses
of vinegary wine, banged with *barras de pan,*
hailing me for being true to my blood,
our fire and our glory, our honor and genius,

as if I'd vanquished Teddy Roosevelt
and his Rough Riders on San Juan Hill,
such a highball rush of Spanishness
that I saw myself as the star attraction
on Columbus Day riding a caravel
down the Gran Vía, dressed in a suit
of lights, crowned with olive leaves,
waving El Cid's sword to the crowds
shouting *¡Viva España! ¡Viva Franco!*

Cervecería Alemana

Among the oldest bars in Madrid
where Hemingway hung out
with bullfighters and anarchists,
it had a wall clock with a dead pendulum,
long iron tables with marble tops
scrubbed daily of soldiers' graffiti,
brass lamps whose soft white light
lured little silver moths at night,
hardwood panels of high polish
meant more for an aristocrat's library
than a place to get loud and drunk.

Speaking fast, walking faster still,
yet with the grace of a dancer,
waiters in white jackets and black ties
wove through the tight spaces,
swerving napping dogs and rucksacks,
their hands turned up as if on tippy-toes,
as they freighted trays of tapas,
espresso cups, glasses and bottles
that stayed straight as stakes
no matter how much they pirouetted.

Nursing our beer drafts for hours
to the chagrin of the waiters
(we tipped well to make amends),
my much older friends and I
would talk and smoke dark tobacco,
Celtas brand, thick twigs inside.
Conversation was quick and loud,
flitting from soccer and girls
to Franco's rule and Basque terrorists,
then just as fast veering off
to the last TV episode of *Kung Fu*

or such Civil War geeky trivia
as that of Republican tank crews
having to use a wood mallet
to shift gears on the Soviet T-26.
Anyone around us, whether young
or old, dapper or slovenly,
would join in with arguments,
vulgar peeves, and the most
excremental blasphemies.

I was just fifteen, but I loved
this chaos of give and take,
a carnival of opinions on the fly,
anarchy of friendship and goodwill
that doesn't translate well into
our American sense of order
and adherence to rules, our creed
of individual responsibility
that makes any slight or faux-pas
rigid and permanent as stone,
so it was a revelation to see Spaniards
forgive the harshest injury
with a *perdón* and good vino.

I Give You Alabanzas, Madrid

O imperial city of convents & discotheques, fiestas & funerals, rogues & mystics,
    I praise—*alabo*—your streets (Gran Vía, Princesa, Alcalá, Montera, Mayor)
      where I strutted at fifteen in plastic high-heel shoes, those flared bell-bottoms
        called elephant legs, my hair puffed like Clapton's on the cover of *Disraeli Gears,*
    how passersby clapped, shouted *Olé* and *Ala, macho!* as I danced on cobblestones,
singing with Lou's junkie tremolo, *How do you think it feels, when you're speeding and lonely.*

Alabo your alley bars, narrow as closets, where we drank beer on tap (Mahou
    or Aguila) and Valdepeñas wine from the barrel, ate tapas of pimento
    olives toothpicked with anchovies, grilled pigs' ears or oil-soaked baby eels,
      your fly-by-night stands where Moroccans with Afros grilled kebabs,
    your grungy dives in Plaza Mayor (or nearby) where chunky women covered in flour
deep-fried calamari for hoagies at midnight, crispiest tentacles money could buy.

Alabo your little boys who sold us squirts of cool water from clay *botijos* those hot
    afternoons when we'd lie down for a siesta on that grassy hill near the river,
    your aproned, wool-slippered old women in winter who roasted chestnuts
      over hot coals sparking like fireflies, your gypsy women in flouncy long skirts
    who sold us red carnations we'd give to the girls in the clubs, petite brunettes
with tiny feet, their platform clogs clopping to *Elected, Diamond Dogs, Frankenstein.*

Alabo your thugs who swaggered in skintight polyester slacks and leather jackets,
    their pockets bulging with pesetas, so they said, but often just balled-up socks,
    your pretty boys feigning toughness with penknives, leather jackets, *quinqui* talk,
      your short-tempered cleaners who fire-hosed the desultory streets, night's debris
    of butts like locust husks, sunflower shells, those curled-up subway tickets
for rolling up hashish with whatever paper we could find (napkin, butcher, bible, etc.).

Alabo your cab drivers who let us jam-pack their small SEAT sedans on our way
    to El Retiro with its quiet ponds and rose gardens for making out at dusk,
    your platoons of drunk soldiers who hugged us as we staggered in the wee hours,
      your night watchmen who kept us safe from thieves when we snoozed on benches,
    waking up to the sung pleas of beggars, then at first light trudging with a hangover
to the bars in Puerta del Sol to eat fresh churros dipped in hot chocolate thick as pudding.

We have lived out years
struggling with sharp winds,
the ancient stench of ruins,
but always there was fruit,
the very simplest,
and there was always a flower.
—HEBERTO PADILLA
     "The Gift" (translated by Alastair Reid
     and Andrew Hurley)

Rasp, Spoon, and Pestle

There were lemons growing old in a clay bowl,
A dozen injured pots that wobbled on the stove,
White countertops with stains like continents

Mamá hid with doilies and patches of an old stole.
A small cabinet stowed vials and jars, her trove
Of ground spices, dry herbs, heirloom condiments

To enchant croquettes, hors d'oeuvres, fillets of sole
Biscay style. With rasp, spoon, and pestle, she strove
To please Papá who scorned those recherché scents

Of haute cuisine, so she fricasseed oxtail in a soul-
Ful red sauce, boiled ham hocks, cooked tripe with cloves
Of garlic—simple, brawny, no buttery ornaments

To make him angry; but on Sundays she'd cajole
Papá with sautés, gratins, and souffles that drove
Him to beg for seconds, thirds, his taste buds in ferment.

Castizo

Centuries ago when the Inquisition
scoured Spain for every secret Jew
or Muslim, people hung sausages,
salted bacon from their thresholds
to prove they were *castizo,*
people of good stock, old Christians
going back three generations.

Blood purity obsessed my mother
not out of pride but rather
from the shame of being impure,
the great-granddaughter
on her mom's side of a Chinese coolie,
making her extol her Catalan father
to the point of believing
he descended from a long line
of hidalgos like Don Quijote,

which leads me to another
Spanish prejudice, the one against
manual labor, also strangely
tied to blood purity. An hidalgo
would never work with his hands
even if it meant wearing rags
and eating cold beans with moldy bread,
as opposed to the moriscos,
Muslim converts, who excelled
in agriculture, manual crafts.

"Don't ever work with your hands,"
Mamá would say. "Go to college.
Become a lawyer or an engineer."
To her a manual worker was ignorant,
brutish, loathsome, no matter how good
a living he might make for his family.

When my father lost his fortune
in the furniture business
and had to go back to being a workman,
a maker of kitchen cabinets,
in a small rented garage near Hialeah,
Mamá lost all respect for him,
complaining of his crude jokes,
rustic manners, hideous farts,
his nasty habit of taking a shower
with his socks and underwear.

"Don't be a failure like your father,"
she'd warn, and though I'd been bookish
from a young age, it was this fear
that nudged me toward college.

Forgive me, Mamá, but all handiwork
is charged with grace. Our hands,
more than our feet, root us to the world.
It is the hand that draws a bird,
scores a requiem, writes an elegy.

Ars Poetica

for my father

At nine you learned to make sofas and chairs
In your uncle's workshop by Havana Bay,
Your pudgy hands, stubby fingers turning
Lithe with wood, cloth, springs, bone, coir,
Your life a reverence to sawdust and burl
As you labored each day in the heat and the light,
Standing on a plank jacked up by bricks,
A ring of tools cuffed to your small wrist,
Your palms and soles callused to stone
As you fluted gadroons, flounced damask,
Beat down unruly tacks to martial rivets.
                                          O *padre mío,*
I learned to craft words watching you sew
With the finest thread and not leave a trace—
To be patient, steadfast, reverent in my work.
Don't dawdle, don't waste, you'd say, but save
What you can't use today for another day:
A scrap of cloth, a stray idea, an orphan verse.
I gazed in wonder as you made the bucksaw
Sway like a violin's bow against strident wood,
How you ironed wrinkled linen to vellum,
Or straightened the crookedest of nails
Because anything can be fixed. Praise you,
Papá, my poet of hammer, needle, and shears.

Heritage

On Sundays when the Father made pancakes,
It was not a quick, light flip of the spatula,
But a throw-down, a smash of batter
Onto the hot cast-iron skillet, his hand a hammer
In a kitchen of crockery and lace curtains
(The Mother gone to Mass in stilettos and a veiled beehive),
So much smoke the sons' eyes winced, throats hacked
As they spooned whipped butter, squirted Aunt Jemima
To a flood, those cratered cakes with hillocks
Of raw flour and rims burnt to cinder *'cause it's ash*
Not sugar that makes you strong, the Father said, *so don't fuss,*
Don't whimper unless you want to eat dirt and mud.
As the sons sat on high stools, legs dangling in rigor,
Underwear baptized in pee, they heard the Father
Talk of their Spanish blood, how it never lies,
Never shames, so pure it can seep through granite
Or dry to rubies in the sun. So don't ever forget,
The Father said, your grandfather and his father before him,
All the way to those first Celts in their stone huts,
And above all our ancient land in the far, far north—
Asturias of the emerald hills, cold rocky rivers, quicksilver clouds,
Where winter rains pummeled the fallen lambs
And the morning fog smothered the sickly trees.
Only the strong-willed survived there, my sons.
Our kin had no need for shoes, a soft bed, or firewood.
Hunger improved their minds, chills toughened their bones,
Icy winds weaned their children from innocence.
Nations die but blood lives forever in *la memoria,*
So pray to your Abuelo as you would God Himself
Who made earth, sky, and water from the void.

My Grandfather the Policeman Takes the Insane to the Asylum

Hershey Train, Matanzas to Havana, 1940s

Fallow cane fields, thatched huts of cutters. Barefoot girls run along the tracks begging for food. Their egret legs sink into the mud. The wind flaps their burlap veils. I'm on the last train to Mazorra where they shock brains, sew lips, geld the young. My Captain warned, *If these locos escape, I promise that your whelps won't eat for a week.* So I've roped them to their seats, put sandbags on their purple feet. How they whimper & drool, their mouths toothless with breath that would wilt the Rose of Jericho. The conductor tells me to gag them, but I say, *No, no, let their tongues speak, bray, or grunt. Don't priests say the insane will inherit the earth?* How they stare at my uniform, stare at my gun, wondering if I am some angel come to earth to take them to heaven. But I am just a simple man, a drunkard, a card player, who barely smiles, takes measly bribes. Where has my innocence gone? Wasn't I once an altar boy, muttering Pater Nosters in my sleep? O, Lord, let me be their deliverer, their apostle, their soul stoker. I hear the wail of Havana's bells, smell her incense of burnt sugar. My will is yours, Father. I will herd this flock to the ramparts on the bay then release them to your holy sea. May the currents guide them to the blueness of Paradise.

Turrón

As with any other Cuban family, our prized
Confection for Christmas Eve was a Spanish nougat
Called *turrón,* whose two traditional types

Are Jijona, a soft, oily paste of honeyed almonds
That must have made St. Teresa levitate
In sinfulness; and Alicante, a wafered brick

Of broken almonds mortared with egg whites
Hard enough to crack a feebly molar. The night
Of Noche Buena, our mahogany table set

With silverware, Spanish linens, Italian glass,
We feasted on Cuban black beans and rice,
Suckling pig, boiled cassava in garlic sauce,

Then right before midnight when angels crow,
Mamá said, she brought out in her taffeta gown
A crystal tray of *turrones,* the crumbly slabs

Laid out like the parquet in our living room
Where votive candles burned around a large
Terracotta Christ Child on a throne of thorns,

His hands, his feet glued with five cloves,
Aromatic *clavos,* same word for nails,
Holy spice that foretells his happy death at 33,

My mother said, how suffering is sweet
In the eyes of God, how blood and tears
Are savorous in Heaven, "so gorge, my son,

Gorge on soft Jijona, his very flesh at Calvary,
And your soul will remain good and clean
A thousand years till Judgment Day."

Sietemesino

Born at seven months
back when most preemies died
without today's high tech
(incubators, ventilators, IV pump, etc.),
I was more like a marsupial
when Mamá took me home—
her little joey, pinkish, shriveled,
barely a kilo, she'd wrap
in oven-warmed blankets
by the kerosene heater.
I suckled fast, hard, insatiably,
hurting her nipples, whose scars
she bore with discreet dignity.
She tapped, poked my chest,
and I never lost my breath.
She made balms from herbs,
boiled so many cod-oil infusions
the nursery smelled like a wharf.
But I grew fat and strong, my head
forested by hazel hair, my chestnut eyes
straight, all my limbs in the right place,
her firstborn son free of brain bleeds,
asthma, jaundice, her miracle baby
destined for great things, so everyone said,
even Chiappi the Italian shopkeeper
on Colmena Avenue who could read
tarot cards, or the Quechua fruit seller
who could discern omens from peels,
or my own Catalan grandfather
who had a dream right before he died
of me as a tall, handsome man riding a horse
on a silver beach with golden skies,
a round city of glass in the distance,
which could portend something wondrous
and profound or nothing at all.

In Memoriam

for my mother, may she rest in peace

Though you could make a mousse or bouillabaisse as good as Julia Child's, your favorite dish was a simple *camarón en escabeche,* shrimp in vinegar marinade, because it reminded you of your birthplace by the sea. We'd sop the cold sauce with flaky Cuban bread and drink Spanish cider from champagne flutes, listening to crackly LPs of boleros and *sones* as we talked about your house in Havana, so close to the bay your young eyes winced in salt air, yet there were always sweet things to eat from street vendors—guava paste, fried dough called *chiviricos,* or those delicious strudels that Polish Jews hawked in Yiddishy Spanish. St. Francis's convent was just a few cobbles away where naughty nuns buried their secrets in tiny tin caskets, you said, and storm tides flooded the streets with evil spirits like the dog-headed fish, the crab-legged cat, harbingers of plagues and corteges, which reminded you of chamber music, so dark, so funereal, you said, because strings are the sinews of sadness. Yet music brought you joy as when you stared through the lacy railings of your balcony at twilight imagining an orchestra playing with prancing peacocks on a flying island, and girls in crinoline gowns who waltzed with princes. Music was your passion from the earliest age when you'd rather sing a carol or a lullaby than jump rope with the girls. At seventeen your father tutored more math students to pay for voice lessons, but on your radio debut you stammered and never got called again, then marriage and motherhood took music's place, and from then on you'd only sing in the shower those haunting arias that I still hear when I think of Havana and the sea. But it saddens me to remember how you often judged your life a failure, your talent wasted, how if you had only had the inner strength to conquer your fears you would've become famous like those divas Olga Guillot and Celia Cruz. Two months before you passed away after having turned 83, you said everything had turned out for the best, that being a mother was a far greater gift for a woman, yet I wonder if you were lying to me (and to yourself), that you had secretly held on to your doubts, your smoldering regrets those many years, and how death stole from you that very last chance at the grace of resolution.

Tortilla Española

Not the corn cake but that thick round omelet
Made with potatoes, onions, and olive oil,
Extra virgin because that's how God wants it
(Add shrimp, tuna, chorizo, red pimientos
For flair), not thin and scrawny as in Cuba,
Mamá said, but a dense wheel of molten yolk
Big as a grindstone, such a staple that all of Spain
Can be heard whipping eggs at dinnertime
Just as our neighbor María José did every night,
A mother of five boys who taught Mamá
How to cook it Castilian style in a deep skillet
Over a slow gas or coal flame, knowing when
To flip la tortilla on a plate so it doesn't overcook
And the egg foams in its bath of fragrant fat,
Those diced potatoes glistening like river pebbles.

Pepe of Plaza Santana

Plaza Santana had three bars, a flamenco club,
a giant chessboard, and Pepe the drunkard
who slept in the bushes surrounding the square,
his winter coat stitched from potato sacks,
a pile of crinkled newspapers his blanket.
The joke was that old Pepe lived *entre plantas,*
literally among the plants, but also the mezzanine
if spelled *entreplanta,* which seems cruel,
though Spanish humor has always been blunt.

Yet there was kindness too as when mothers
gave Pepe slabs of tortilla or their children
big bags of sunflower seeds in the shell,
though he had no front teeth to crack them with.
Whenever the tapas crowds gave him coins,
he'd quickly buy wine in short *chatos,* tall *cañas,*
but mostly he relied on hand-me-down bottles
of dreggy *tintos,* sour sangrias, even those dry
cooking wines loaded with salt. One time
Pepe got so skinny that the barkeepers
themselves spooned egg soup into his mouth.
One very cold day the groundskeeper let him
sleep in the chess shed, and it remained his home
for many months until the ambulance men
gurneyed him away past the staring players.

Whether he was dead or just sick no one knew.
Some spoke of God's mercy, others cold fate,
and though there was pity, no one thought
he was the victim of a disease called alcoholism.
It was all a matter of excess in a culture
where eating and drinking were sacramental,
so that breaking bread with wine was civilized

but dining with plain water was beastly.
Children drank not milk but house wine
mixed with lemon soda, and any mother
squirting brandy into a cup of hot milk
with Nescafé had no fear the nuns would take
her brood to an orphanage since Christ
himself got tipsy at the Last Supper
knowing he had just a few hours to enjoy
those last red drops from the jug.

Good Friday in Madrid

> Mothers of America
> let your kids go to the movies!
> —FRANK O'HARA, "Ave Maria"

The whole city shut down in mourning
(cops on the lookout for drunkards
and hash smokers), there was nothing to do
except join a procession with boys
who wear saints' medals like cowbells
and smell of rancid olive oil or see
a religious movie in black and white
with lots of crying to even weepier violins.
But I found this one theater near San Bernardo
showing *El Cid,* so I paid the matinee
price of ten pesetas to see Charlton Heston
play the greatest warrior of all time
with Sophia Loren as the damsel Ximena.
I loved the battle scenes, the Moors'
swirly costumes, the Andalusian horses
with their shiny coats. Heston made a perfect hero
clenching his teeth tight as iron grates,
shaking the earth as he stomped against his enemies,
smashing them with a sword big as a lamppost.
Papá says Heston's a man's man, so he must hate
vegetables, eat raw meat, drive a Gran Torino,
but he's surely the worst lover in Hollywood.
I couldn't believe how he didn't drool at the sight
of Sophia Loren, the most beautiful woman
in the galaxy. I would've sweated, trembled all over
touching those beige arms, that thick black hair.
He was standoffish, stiffer than a rubber mallet
whenever she tried to kiss him. Was it garlic breath?
Impossible. I would've stuck my lips to hers

with crazy glue or soldered them together
for eternity. I would've been Sophia's remora,
Sophia's tapeworm, even a mole on her neck,
or her loneliest little uvula wiggling every time
she said *caro mio, biscottino, ti amo amore mio.*

Fuego

When fascists ruled and churchmen stifled sex,
Lonely boys, workers' sons, secret anarchists,
Found love in moonlit alleys and porticos,
Women in silver beehives and black stilettos
Who'd ask for *fuego,* spark to light a Ducado
And talk of how young you are and let us go
Drink gin in sawdust bars by the blue hotel.
I'll teach you to slurp mussels from the shell.
I'll teach you to suck honey from the gloom.
Let us flee the rising sun in my attic room
Where roses blaze, jasmine blooms in the wet
Night air. Breathe my breath, lick my sweat.
Let hands strum your thighs, lips tattoo your skin.
Blessèd you'll be as dry earth that gets the rain.

Letter to the Generalissimo

Dearest Caudillo, did your bursts of gunpowder
shake the firmament when you shot down
those 5,000 partridges on a warm summer day?
You were then in your late sixties, a tad old and creaky
but certainly not infirm (or infamous,
for that matter), so you were proud that no other
general had held up your barrel or whispered
in your good ear where to aim in the sneaky sky.
With God's help no shell went flat. The dogs
did not slobber. The water carrier knew
how to clap reverently as the Minister of War
exalted your prowess, comparing you
to El Cid Campeador and Santiago the Moorslayer.
But tell me, Pancho, did you really have to kill
all those little birds? They were no threat
to your manhood or to the state. It's not as if
they were Marxists on the rampage in Madrid.
You could have just interned them in a camp
with bare concrete, no bushes to hide, their legs
weighed down with lead, an electric fence to zap
little beaks too inquisitive for their own good.

The Day Admiral Carrero Blanco Died

On that Thursday right before Christmas
when Spaniards carol to the tabor,
crack walnuts and filberts by the crèche,
Franco's prime minister and successor
blew up in his chauffeured limousine
as he went to work after morning Mass.
Basque terrorists from ETA had planted
a 100-pound bomb under the street,
rocketing the admiral five stories high.
Days of mourning soon followed.
Classes were canceled. Cinemas closed.
Civil Guards clutched machine guns
in the metro, plazas, and on street corners.
That Saturday as I walked up Carretas
to meet my friends at Punto y Coma Café,
fear suffused the cold air like a fog
or mist that seeped into one's bones,
blanched one's face to candle wax,
those few passersby around me
flimsy as marionettes in the chapping wind.
Somewhere (or anywhere) I am sure
Marxists were being rubber-hosed on their knees,
hippies forced to eat their protest songs,
college students dunked into icy water,
but my parents, our neighbors, our friends—
all the shopkeepers, bureaucrats, priests—
prayed for martial law, El Caudillo riding
his horse of vengeance into the streets
because any commotion can lead to another
takeover by the communists who'll burn
churches, rape nuns, desecrate saints,
turn our children to godless Bolsheviks.

Across the centuries,
through the world's nothingness
sleepless I seek you.
—RAFAEL ALBERTI
"Paradise Lost" (translated by
Christopher Sawyer-Lauçanno)

Through the plain, through the wind,
black pony, red moon.
Death is looking at me
from the towers of Córdoba.
—FEDERICO GARCÍA LORCA
"Rider's Song" (translated by
Stephen Spender and J. L. Gili)

Madrid in the Civil War

As if painted in thermite aquarelles,
Winds gyre in the throes of blitzkrieg;
Tram cars burn and twist like viscera;
Donkeys and mules bloat to zeppelins.

But the city remains stubborn against
The bullets, the bombs, the mortars.
Wrens build nests in the holes of a belfry

Whose battered bell stutters the Angelus,
And boys without bread begin their day
Baking balls of sawdust leavened with mud;

Ragged girls sew gowns from the parachutes
Of Germans shot by snub-nosed Polikarpovs,
Corpses bartered for bails of mildewed wurst.

Mothers crouch with their newborns
Behind the barricades of charred pews,
Kitchen knives strapped to their garters,
So many, so many raped by Franco's soldiers.

O tell me Condor legionnaire
What is in your heart as your Heinkel
Drops incendiaries on women
Returning from market with empty baskets?

What thoughts propel
Through your mind as you strafe
The children playing jacks
In their cratered schoolyard?

You answer, "I feel the will to power.
War is an art, and art itself is war
Against morality, against reason,
Against the mediocre mind
That fails to see beauty in destruction."

You invoke Bosch and Brueghel
As visionaries who understood
How the gun is mightier than the brush,
How the sounds of war are music
To the seraphim, highest among angels.

I call you a liar, a cynic, a fraud.
How ingenious you are at ransacking
Sublime words to consecrate murder.
Art is love, I say. Art is God in the flesh.

Jacob's Angel told me so. I wrestled him well.
I raced up his ladder to heaven. "Build cathedrals
From the bricks of hate," he said. "Let the blood
Of innocents surge into life's waters, so many rivers,
So many creeks to feed the fields of our Lord."

An American Nurse at the Battle of Teruel

December of 1937

It gets so cold at night it hurts to breathe, but there are no more chairs and doors to burn. The clocks have no hands, the church bells melted down for bullets. The dead get thrown into a wishing well, and I hear their bones crack against the stony water. I see the ghosts of children ice-skating on ponds of blood. How happy they are, unlike the living who hide in root cellars, fighting off the rats and one another. Our doctor got killed the other day rummaging the rubble for canned fish, and I am alone among the wounded. The gauze is gone, so dirt will have to do. The alcohol, too, which soldiers steal to drink for warmth. Frostbite plagues the men in the trenches of ice, their hands and feet mummified, but what can I do with a dull saw, a rusty bayonet for a scalpel. Why have You, my God, sent us blizzards and not the gentle snow of Christmas? Should we hang grenades from scorched trees? Should we carve nativities from weathered bones? I have seen how puss runs down to icicles from wounds of the newly dead whose eyes stare at me like the stars of Bethlehem.

Federico García Lorca

That August day
in an olive grove
south of Granada,
those fascists
who gunned you down

(men who dream
of sundering the stars,
bombing the moon,
cudgeling the clouds)

could not stomp
your beautiful words
into hate's mire,

could not garrote
your green guitar
into silence,

could not sink
your caravels
of verse that glide
the syllabled seas.

That August day
in an olive grove
south of Granada,
Doña Muerte
took your hand
like a *bailadora*
in frills of carnation,
spikenard heels,
and you danced
to El Paraíso

on jasmine clouds,
sunrays of lemon rind,
a thousand duendes
blowing bulls' horns,
rattling the rubies
of pomegranate maracas,
their cantos so vibrant
in the saffron air
they strummed the limbs
of your orange trees
to airs of cante jondo.

Valley of the Fallen

All the mothers of the world
hide their bellies . . .
—MIGUEL HERNÁNDEZ, "War"

In the Guadarrama Mountains outside Madrid,
a Latin cross, 200,000 tons, 150 meters high,
impales an outcrop like a sword thrust into a bull's neck,
& below this poor beast, Franco's basilica crouches
in the dark, larger than St. Peter's in Rome, eighteen years to build,
with gothic vaults, a massive nave, crypts for the fascist dead.

O guiltless mountain disemboweled & butchered,
your every tree, bush, flower, weed, root, moss, bud, tendril & leaf
corrupted to build this temple for Franco's fallen,
his legionnaires, his henchmen, his blue shirts, his red berets, his priests
in armored chasubles who killed & maimed in God's name,
without mercy to their enemies, without honor to their wives,
without consolation to their orphaned children.

O innocent España tortured & helpless,
your new caudillo Francisco Franco, crusader of crusaders,
God's right hand, commanded that fourteen chapels
be carved from granite, most blessed stone, bone from heaven,
his monument to the yoke & the arrows, the eagle turned vulture,
the angels who fired on farmers, the saints who rammed
tanks on the houses of the poor, the four evangelists who flew
the bombers that blasted Guernica to smithereens.

O innocent prisoners desolate & afraid—
students, laborers, plowmen, factory workers, sailors, actors—
españoles who took up arms to bring justice to *la patria*—
be you communists, socialists, anarchists, or atheists, I do not care,
who toiled with shovel & pike, chisel & hammer,
sledge & dynamite, with little water, little food, scant shelter
for one man's pride, one man's glory, one man's vainglorious destiny
to outlast the three Philips, even Ferdinand & Isabella.

O martyrs of the good & the humble sacred,
so many of you, between 30,000 and 80,000, lying beneath the slabs,
beneath the trees, beneath the patches of weed,
without marker, without cairn, without the simplest cross,
may this poem bring you even one grain of grace.

ACKNOWLEDGMENTS

Some of the poems in this book first appeared in the following publications, sometimes in earlier forms and with different titles: *Chelsea:* "Doctor Lu"; *Crab Orchard Review:* "Macho"; *Huizache:* "Fuego" and "Tortilla Española"; *Los Angeles Review:* "Sharing a Meal with the Cuban Ex-Political Prisoners"; *New Letters:* "Kissing in Madrid"; *Pilgrimage Magazine:* "My Father's Pantry"; *Potomac Review:* "Rock 'n' Roll Animal"; and *Southern Review:* "Ars Poetica" and "Rasp, Spoon, and Pestle."

"Kissing in Madrid" also appeared in *Not Like the Rest of Us: An Anthology of Contemporary Indiana Authors,* ed. Barbara Shoup and Rachel Sahaidachny (Indiana Writers Center, 2016).

"El Rastro" appeared as a "Poem-a-Day" on October 4, 2018, on the website of the Academy of American Poets.

Rafael Alberti, excerpt from *The Lost Grove.* Republished with permission of the University of California Press—Books, from *The Lost Grove,* by Rafael Alberti. Copyright © 1976 by The Regents of the University of California; permission conveyed through Copyright Clearance Center, Inc.

Rafael Alberti, excerpt from "Paradise Lost" translated by Christopher Sawyer-Lauçanno, from *Concerning the Angels.* Copyright 1928, © 1995 by Rafael Alberti. Translation copyright © 1995 by Christopher Sawyer-Lauçanno. Reprinted with the permission of The Permissions Company, Inc., on behalf of City Lights Books, www.citylights.com.

Philip Larkin, excerpt from "This Be the Verse" from *Collected Poems.* Copyright © 2003. Reprinted with permission of Farrar, Straus and Giroux and Faber and Faber Ltd.

"Song of the Rider" by Federico García Lorca, translated by Stephen Spender and J. L. Gili, from *The Selected Poems of Federico García Lorca,* copyright © 1955 by

NOTES

"Kissing in Madrid"

My family moved from Miami to Madrid, Spain, in 1973, where my father had bought a furniture store off Marqués de Urquijo near the Argüelles metro stop. As Cubans with Spanish fathers, my parents felt a special fondness for España. Nonetheless, when the business failed two years later, we returned to Miami to live in the exile community once again.

"Macho"

In the middle to late 1960s, the Castro government set up labor camps in the countryside to intern antirevolutionary elements, specifically men unwilling or proscribed from doing military service. Among these were homosexual men. These camps went by the acronym UMAP (Unidades Militares de Ayuda a la Producción), or Military Units to Assist in Production.

"Camp"

This curious fact about the Spanish Civil War that begins the poem is taken from Antony Beevor's *The Battle for Spain: The Spanish Civil War, 1936–1939* (Penguin, 2006), page 124.

"Matador"

This poem was inspired by the life of the Spanish bullfighter Juan Belmonte (1892–1962) as told to the journalist Manuel Chaves Nogales in his book *Juan Belmonte, matador de toros: Su vida y sus hazañas* (Libros del Asteroide, 2009).

"The Man with No Name"

A little-known fact about Sergio Leone's spaghetti westerns is that they were shot in the south of Spain.

"Judo"

A "cubanazo" is a tough-guy, rednecky kind of Cuban.

"Pirates World"

Pirates World was an amusement park with, as the name indicates, many pirate-themed rides, besides being a popular venue for rock concerts. It opened in 1967 and closed in 1975.

"Rock 'n' Roll Animal"

The lyrics that end the poem are from Lou Reed's "Heroin," first recorded with the Velvet Underground in their debut album *The Velvet Underground and Nico* (1967).

Autostop

A *cornudo* is a cuckold.

"Talking to Lou Reed: A Boy's Homage"

The italicized words and lines are from the lyrics of various songs by Lou Reed, with or without the Velvet Underground, in the following order: "Vicious," "Heroin," "Lisa Says," "Sad Song," "Berlin," "Perfect Day," and "I'm Waiting for the Man." The legionnaires are the *legionarios* of La Legión Española (the Spanish Legion), an elite fighting unit (one of its mottoes being "Hail to Death") founded in the 1920s by José Millán Astray, a flamboyant Spanish general of fascist leanings.

"I Give You Alabanzas, Madrid"

The lyric that ends the first stanza is from Lou Reed's song "How Do You Think It Feels" from the album *Berlin* (1972). The *quinquis* were juvenile delinquents whose argot used many words from caló, the language of the Romas in Spain, such as *menda* for "guy," *gachí* for "girl," etc.

"Sietemesino"

My father and my mother, already pregnant with me, left Cuba for Lima, Peru, in 1957, where I was born quite prematurely in 1958. When I was ten years old, we moved to Miami, where I then grew up on Coral Reef Drive and in Little Havana. I thus consider myself Cuban-American.

"Letter to the Generalissimo"

I learned about Franco's supposed prowess as a hunter reading Antonio Cazorla Sánchez's *Franco: The Biography of the Myth* (Routledge, 2014), specifically page 173.

"An American Nurse at the Battle of Teruel"

The source and inspiration for this poem is *Into the Fire: American Women in the Spanish Civil War,* a documentary film from 2002 directed by Julia Newman.

"Valley of the Fallen"

La patria can be translated as the motherland or the fatherland, depending on one's political leanings.

CPSIA information can be obtained
at www.ICGtesting.com
Printed in the USA
LVHW090804310119
605582LV00011B/5/P

"*Memoria* carries us from Miami to Madrid, to 'where every road and every life begins and ends,' exploring feelings of exile and definitions of being a man (*macho*) imposed by family, religion, and culture. Castro, Franco, Lou Reed, and other figures become a whetstone for the narrator's burgeoning self. Delivering an impressive array of sonnets, odes, elegies, prose poems, and more, Menes unpacks the relationship between memory and its kin: identity. *Memoria* is a tour-de-force of form and feeling."

—Shara McCallum

"When Orlando Ricardo Menes is at his best, and he is rarely not, he writes into the spiritual, the familial, the sexual, the sensual, the quotidian, that I find myself thinking: we need more poetry like this. His sense of line and language are superb. His eye for what ought to be obvious, a terrifying pleasure. His ear for how we hear, perhaps terrifyingly and pleasurably more so. *Memoria* is nothing more than a gift."

—Mark Statman

BORN to Cuban parents in Lima, Perú, raised in Miami among political exiles, and having spent two years in Francoist Spain, Orlando Ricardo Menes pays tribute to the resilience and tradition that shape Hispanic culture across the globe while critiquing the hypermasculine characteristics embedded within. Ripe with pride and shame, beauty and aversion, *Memoria* relays the personal path one takes while navigating the complexities of heritage.

MICHAEL WIENS

ORLANDO RICARDO MENES is a Cuban-American writer who was born in Lima, Perú. A professor of English at the University of Notre Dame, he is the author of six poetry collections and the poetry editor of the *Notre Dame Review*.

LSU Press
Baton Rouge 70803
www.lsupress.org

COVER DESIGN BY
MANDY MCDONALD SCALLAN

ISBN: 978-0-8071-6941-4

90000 >

9 780807 169414